For Peter Pan

on her

70th birthday

# For Peter Pan

## on her

# 70th birthday

A PLAY

## Sarah Ruhl

THEATRE COMMUNICATIONS GROUP
NEW YORK
2018

The publication of *For Peter Pan on her 70th birthday* by Sarah Ruhl, through TCG's Book Program, is made possible in part by the New York State Council on the Arts with the support of Governor Andrew Cuomo and the New York State Legislature.

TCG books are exclusively distributed to the book trade by Consortium Book Sales and Distribution.

ISBN 978-1-55936-559-8 (paperback)
ISBN 978-1-55936-879-7 (ebook)

A catalog record for this book is available from the Library of Congress.

Book design and composition by Lisa Govan
Cover design by Monet Cogbill
Cover photo of the author's mother in *Peter Pan*, Davenport, Iowa.
Courtesy of Kathleen Kehoe Ruhl.

First Edition, May 2018

*For Kathleen Kehoe Ruhl. Happy belated birthday.*
*With thanks to J. M. Barrie.*
*With love and great gratitude to the Kehoes.*

# Contents

# FOREWORD

*B*efore Sarah Ruhl could write she told stories to her attentive mother, Kathleen, who typed them up. (In those days, in the late seventies, Kathleen, who now has a PhD in Language, Literacy and Rhetoric, was a high-school English teacher, moonlighting as an actress and theater director.) "Vivid" is one adjective that Ruhl uses to describe her. Kathleen was known to serve up dinner while delivering the maid's speech from *The Bald Soprano* and to organize Pig Night: she inculcated good table manners in her two daughters by allowing them to be horrible at dinner once a week. "We were encouraged to play at home, so that art-making didn't seem like an escape from family or a retreat but very much a part of life," Ruhl recalled. Ruhl's play *For Peter Pan on her 70th birthday* is a droll, elegiac homage to her actress-mother's spirited playfulness and to the loving Midwestern family from which she emerged. (In 2017, Kathleen appeared in the Shattered Globe Theatre production of the work in Chicago.) It is also a testament to the slyness of Ruhl's civility and her stagecraft.

Ruhl calls *For Peter Pan* a "Midwestern Noh drama." The play
borrows the three-part Noh structure and also contends with
ancestors—in the shape of George, the dying father of the five
children we meet at his hospital bedside, whose spirit follows
the disputatious clan from death watch to wake. Ruhl's story is
also underpinned by Noh drama's psychological strategy. "The
protagonist meets the ghost, then recognizes the ghost, then
dances with or embraces the ghost," Ruhl writes, a clue to the
paradoxical game of loss and reparation she is playing. *For Peter
Pan* elegantly navigates its audience through the multiple space-
time realities of consciousness: past, present, and time-out-of-
time—the mythic realm of play. At once a mourning and a cel-
ebration, a ghost story and a love story, a meditation on death
and an assertion of the triumph of imagination over time, the
play invokes a kind of double haunting, in which Ruhl haunts
her family story as it continues to haunt her. "To me," she writes
of her large extended Irish-Catholic Iowa family, "they were the
cradle of civilization, my own Mesopotamia."

*For Peter Pan* conjures both the music of Time and the music
of the Ruhl family's palaver. It's organized in movements, not
acts—a kind of symphony of history and fantasy. At curtain rise,
Ann speaks to us directly—"Hello. I play Pan" are her first words—
recalling the thrill of her performance when she was a young girl
in Davenport, Iowa. "I wasn't ever scared to fly in the theater,"
she says, adding, "it was after I had children I was afraid to fly."
The last movement of the play transports her as an adult back to
Neverland, and to that never-forgotten youthful performance, in
which she was gravity's angel, flying free. Only now, Ann's own
siblings have become the Darling family, bringing their earthly
issues into the kingdom of make-believe. Backstage after the
show, Ann also reencounters her dead father, as he was then,
existing in the theater's disconcerting liminal space between
ordinary and extraordinary worlds.

PETER PAN: I'm suddenly afraid.
    Did you die?
    What was it like?
    Your breathing was terrible.
    It seemed like you didn't want to go.
    Was it awful?
GEORGE: Come on now, change your costume.

The pulse of Ruhl's melancholy heart is powerfully felt beneath the understatement of this stage-managed resurrection. The dead have no answers; however, they do have presence. Among the many suggestive ideas the play captures is the presence of this absence in daily life. *For Peter Pan* moves between the diurnal and the spiritual, lightly contending with death in order to befriend it. Ruhl's plays always mix grief with gladness. She understands that without shadow there is no brilliance. Here, Peter Pan, being a sprite, has lost his shadow: he is not corporeal and therefore isn't bound by the laws of gravity, which propel Homo sapiens downward and deathward. Ruhl has fun with this contradiction.

WENDY: Everything has a shadow, Peter Pan. Honestly you
    should have gone to Jungian analysis. You would have
    learned that you can't experience joy without your
    dark side.
PETER PAN: I don't know what you just said, Wendy.
WENDY: You can live on Freud until you're forty but when
    you're seventy and facing death you either need reli-
    gion or Carl Jung.
PETER PAN: Why can't I fly without my shadow?
JOHN: Think about it, Peter.
PETER PAN: What?
JOHN: A plane that's flying without its shadow on the
    ground is—
PETER PAN: Is what—

*John makes the sound of an explosion.*

JOHN: Poof—dead!
PETER PAN: Or just flying at night!
WENDY: I've sewn it on, Peter.
PETER PAN: Oh, well done! It's on again, my shadow is on again!

*She crows.*

Now I can fly!

*She's not hooked into any flying apparatus.*
*She tries to fly, does a little jump.*

JOHN: That was the worst flying I ever saw, Peter.

In Ruhl's Neverland slapstick replaces sentimentality and everyone seems more or less grounded. Peter can't get lift-off. Likewise, bitching about panic attacks, diabetes, and other ailments of age, the family struggles with the proposition of being both outside of temporal existence and claimed by it. Captain Hook, who is called out as a bully during the evening, humiliates Peter for his failure to fly, for his exposure as a mere fairy-tale pedestrian.

HOOK: Heard a rumor you walked here, Pan. Why didn't you fly?
PETER PAN: You must be mistaken. I flew.
HOOK: No, Peter Pan. You thought you'd never grow up. But you have. You walked here. Slowly.

These are fighting words. They duel. "Who are you?" Hook taunts. "I am youth. I am joy," Peter insists. "Then fly," Hook brays, finally putting his sword to Peter's neck and killing him. Peter is literally laid low; gravity seems to have won the day. But Ruhl and Peter Pan are all about lightness of style: aided by Tinker Bell's fairy dust, Peter is clapped back to life by the audience. He flies, finally.

JOHN: Annie, you're flying! You're really flying!
PETER PAN: I'm not Ann—
    I'm Pan!
    Peter Pan!

*She crows.*

WENDY: Peter! What was death like?
MICHAEL: Does consciousness persist after all?
PETER PAN: It was flying! It was wonderful!

*She crows.*

Oh I'm light!
Light as air!

"My hope was that every time Peter Pan died in this play and the audience resurrected her by clapping, my mother would live forever," Ruhl writes in the Preface. But, as her play dramatizes, the true resurrection is that of the human imagination itself, which has the power to kill Time and redeem the actual with the magical.

Not long ago, when she was down in the dumps, Ruhl wrote out for herself a list of the reasons that she writes. One of the twenty-five was "Write for the present, but sideways." *For Peter Pan*, which celebrates imaginative freedom, addresses a terrorized society, gripped by a passion for ignorance. By coaxing the public to think outside the box, *For Peter Pan*, in its oblique way, calls out the culture's psychic numbness. How do we shift the things that weigh us down? How do we find the courage to defy fear? How do we make our joy? These questions are hard to hear in our barbarous era which clamors for sensation without penetration. They are even harder to answer. Most of the theatrical stories we tell ourselves these days are noisier, more lurid, more violent, a sort of strip-mining of sensibility. "I've started to feel that putting a moment of gentleness onstage is a radical political act," Ruhl, who uses a softer theatrical palette for her effects, said.

Maybe because I am old now, and still long to fly, *For Peter Pan* never fails to move me to tears. I cried the first time I read the play a few years ago on a plane somewhere over Colorado. I cried last night when I read it again at home in London. What is it about the play, beyond that yearning to transcend the limits of mind and body, that is so affecting? It's something about the generosity of Ruhl's spirit, which comes through the deftness of the play's design: her faith in beauty; her poetic economy of phrase; her gratitude for the living and the dead; her wonder at the mighty mystery of things.

—*John Lahr*
*London*
*January 2018*

# PREFACE

*I* wrote *For Peter Pan on her 70th birthday* as a gift for my mother (for her seventieth birthday). My mother grew up playing Peter Pan in Davenport, Iowa. As a child I looked at pictures scattered around my grandparents' house of my mother wearing green tights and flying. One picture even had Mary Martin's arm around my beaming mother. Mary Martin had come through Davenport, Iowa, on a national tour. The local paper set up a meeting between their local Peter Pan (my teenaged mother) and Mary Martin in her dressing room, with a photo opportunity. My mother was so nervous that she forgot her *Peter Pan* script in Mary Martin's dressing room, so Mary Martin sent it back signed, with a bouquet of flowers.

And so in my young mind, *Peter Pan* was conflated with my mother, who embodied the magic of theater. My mother was always someone who had an ambivalent relationship with the word "grown-up," and she's always stayed young, in the sense of being devoted, playful, and very much alive, in the theater. My mother was always acting in some play or another during my childhood in Chicago, and I would accompany her to small darkened theaters, sitting in the back, and taking notes. My mother still acts. (As a matter of fact, she just played a version of herself in *For Peter Pan* in Chicago. I thought the world might implode in the Borgesian sense when my mother played a version of my mother. But it did not explode. For me, it got a little bigger.)

My mother took a break from acting when my father grew sick and died at the age of fifty-two. She lost my father, then her mother and father, in quick succession, nursing each of them through cancer. By one definition, you grow up when your parents die. So it's perhaps fitting that I set this play on the eve of the family patriarch's death.

I have a large extended Irish-Catholic family from Iowa that has always been, to me, the cradle of civilization. My own Mesopotamia is found along the banks of the Mississippi River in the Quad Cities, where I spent every holiday, catching fireflies with cousins, reading books all day while dipping my hand into a jar of homemade party mix, rolling down hills, lighting sparklers, and eating ham. I also spent my holidays in Iowa listening to people who love each other argue about politics.

At some point I grew up, refused to eat ham, and argued with the people I love about politics. It is a family sport. It was a family sport that climaxed in the Clinton years, when the right and left were polarized in a new way, then got more hostile in the Bush years, and is starting to wane now, as we find we can no longer talk to each other across party lines. So we talk to each other about anything and everything but politics. And in the privacy of our own homes, we watch different news channels on TV. I love and adore my family. Part of what I tried to capture or preserve in the play (for myself as much as anyone) was a certain musicality of speech when a family of five is talking. J. M. Barrie wrote, in his preface to *Peter Pan*, to the five children he wrote the play for: "I suppose I always knew that I made Peter by rubbing the five of you violently together . . . that is all he is, the spark I got from you."

When I learned that Barrie wrote *Peter Pan* by rubbing five people he loved together, I felt less worried about writing a play by rubbing five people I love together. Because I was writing about living people with real histories (though their avatars are composite and fictional), I interviewed my extended family for the process, passed drafts by them, and courted their feedback. As I wrote the play, I called my characters 1 through 5 on the page, by birth order, as Barrie did—because I was more interested in the musicality of speech and polyphony that comes from a hive mind than I was in individuation. I wondered if it was possible to write a play about one's family without it being a "family drama" of the sort that hinges on mudslinging and skeletons in the closet. I wondered if it was possible to write a play about one's family with love, a play they might want to come see. Rather than hinging the play structurally on a buried or invented secret, I used a dramatic structure that approximated Japanese Noh drama, which has a three-part structure: the protagonist meets the ghost, then recognizes the ghost, then dances with or embraces the ghost. One might imagine this structure as a contemporary Midwestern Noh drama.

When I teach playwriting at Yale School of Drama, I often ask my students to begin by writing a personal "gift play" to another student. I pair them, have them interview their recipient, and write short plays, which they present in an intimate setting. I was inspired to do this by Lewis Hyde, who argues in his seminal book, *The Gift*, that, "A gift that cannot be given away ceases to be a gift." Hyde's central theme is how artists survive in a capitalist economy, when the seeds of their art are actually much more firmly and naturally rooted in a gift economy. What his book taught me was how to keep looking for intrinsic reasons to make theater, rather than looking to the marketplace. Giving a gift to my mother and my extended family continues to be one of my favorite reasons to write a play. I thank them for receiving it. My hope was that every time Peter Pan died in this play and the audience resurrected her by clapping, my mother would live forever.

*—Sarah Ruhl*
*New York City*
*August 2017*

What I want to do first is to give Peter to the Five without whom he never would have existed. I hope, my dear sirs, that in memory of what we have been to each other you will accept this dedication with your friends love . . . I suppose I always knew that I made Peter by rubbing the five of you violently together . . . that is all he is, the spark I got from you . . . My grandest triumph, the best thing in the play of Peter Pan (though it is not in it), is that long after No. 4 had ceased to believe [in fairies], I brought him back to the faith for at least two minutes . . .

—J. M. Barrie, a dedication, preface to Peter Pan

For Peter Pan

on her

70th birthday

## PRODUCTION HISTORY

*For Peter Pan on her 70th birthday* had its world premiere at Actors Theatre of Louisville (Les Waters, Artistic Director; Jennifer Bielstein, Managing Director) as part of the 40th Humana Festival of New American Plays, on March 8, 2016. It was directed by Les Waters. The scenic design was by Annie Smart, the costume design was by Kristopher Castle, the lighting design was by Matthew Frey, the sound design was by Bray Poor; the dramaturg was Amy Wegener and the production stage manager was Paul Mills Holmes. The cast was:

| | |
|---|---|
| Kathleen Chalfant | ANN/1 |
| Scott Jaeck | JOHN/2 |
| David Chandler | JIM/3 |
| Keith Reddin | MICHAEL/4 |
| Lisa Emery | WENDY/5 |
| Ron Crawford | GEORGE |

*For Peter Pan on her 70th birthday* had its West Coast premiere at Berkeley Repertory Theatre (Tony Taccone, Artistic Director; Susan Medak, Managing Director) on May 20, 2016. It was directed by Les Waters. The scenic design was by Annie Smart, the costume design was by Kristopher Castle, the lighting design was by Matthew Frey, the sound design was by Bray Poor; the dramaturg was Amy Wegener and the production stage manager was Michael Suenkel. The cast was:

| Kathleen Chalfant | ANN/1 |
| Charles Shaw Robinson | JOHN/2 |
| David Chandler | JIM/3 |
| Keith Reddin | MICHAEL/4 |
| Ellen McLaughlin | WENDY/5 |
| Ron Crawford | GEORGE |
| Yodel | A DOG |

*For Peter Pan on her 70th birthday* had its Chicago premiere at Shattered Globe Theatre (Sandy Shinner, Producing Artistic Director; Doug McDade, Managing Director) on April 6, 2017. It was directed by Jessica Thebus. The scenic design was by Jack Magaw, the costume design was by Sarah Jo White, the lighting design was by Shelley Strasser Holland, the sound design was by Christopher Kriz, the projection design was by Michael Stanfill; the stage manager was Tina Jach. The cast was:

| Kathleen Ruhl | ANN/1 |
| HB Ward | JOHN/2 |
| Ben Werling | JIM/3 |
| Patrick Thornton | MICHAEL/4 |
| Eileen Niccolai | WENDY/5 |
| Doug McDade | GEORGE |

*For Peter Pan on her 70th birthday* had its New York premiere at Playwrights Horizons (Tim Sanford, Artistic Director; Leslie Marcus, Managing Director) on August 18, 2017. It was directed by Les Waters. The scenic design was by David Zinn, the costume design was by Kristopher Castle, the lighting design was by Matt Frey, the sound design and original music were by Charles Coes and Bray Poor; the production stage manager was Amanda Spooner. The cast was:

| | |
|---|---|
| Kathleen Chalfant | ANN/1 |
| Daniel Jenkins | JOHN/2 |
| David Chandler | JIM/3 |
| Keith Reddin | MICHAEL/4 |
| Lisa Emery | WENDY/5 |
| Ron Crawford | GEORGE |
| Macy | A DOG |

## CHARACTERS

Five siblings from a close-knit family, two women and three men.
They are numbered according to birth order: 1, 2, 3, 4, 5.
All love their family. Most love to fight about politics. All from
Iowa.

1—Ann, between sixty and seventy. Plays Peter Pan.
2—John, in his late sixties. Plays John in *Peter Pan*.
3—Jim, in his mid-sixties. Plays Captain James Hook in *Peter Pan*.
4—Michael, in his early sixties. Plays Michael in *Peter Pan*.
5—Wendy, in her late fifties. Plays Wendy in *Peter Pan*.
    George, in his eighties. In Movement One, a dying man; in
    Movement Two, a ghost; in Movement Three, himself.
    Oh—and a dog. A real dog. If possible.


## SET

1. The theater.
2. A hospital room: an empty space with a white curtain, a spare
   rolling bed, a white sheet, and some chairs.
3. A breakfast nook: an empty space with a round rolling table,
   a yellow lamp overhead, and some chairs.
4. Neverland: an empty space with painted backdrops that fly in.
5. The theater.

If there is no actual flying, one can imagine beautiful painted backdrops that help give us the sensation of flight. In the Chicago production, for example, a simple white sheet was hung on a clothesline, and Victorian scrolling panoramas and magic lantern projections were used to good effect. The effects should feel childlike and handmade rather than slick. If actors are not rigged to fly, but a stage direction calls for flight, let the actors simply *believe* that they are flying . . . believing in flight seems to work better than pretending to be flying.

## TIME

Sometime in the Clinton era.
And in the land of memory.
And Neverland, which has no time.

## NOTES

Dialogue sometimes lacks capitalization or punctuation when it seems as though the characters are finishing each other's sentences. There is a certain musicality of speech when a family of five is talking. Some of the dialogue in Movement Two is taken from interviews with my extended family.
Movements One and Two should feel almost unperformed. (Movement One is waiting, Movement Two is remembering, Movement Three is going.)
Movement Three should often feel like full-on children's theater, arms akimbo, with real people hovering underneath their roles in *Peter Pan*.

# PROLOGUE

*Ann/1, a woman between sixty and seventy years of age, enters in front of a curtain.*
*She holds a crumpled yellowed program.*

1

*(To the audience)* Hello.
I'll be playing Peter Pan.
*(Reading her program)* This is something of a relic.
Peter Pan, presented by the Davenport Children's Theatre in Davenport, Iowa, 1955.

Let's see . . . *(Reading the program)* Mr. Smee—played by Bump Heeter. Tinker Bell—played by herself, of course. Mrs. Darling—Mary Ellen Hurlbutt—oh my God she was in my wedding. When she was still a Hurlbutt. We used to call her Fling Fanny.

Our first production was at the Shriner's temple, a big building on Brady Street, where the Shriners did mysterious things. Then we upgraded to the Orpheum, a real movie theater, where Mary Martin once performed. I met her when she came through town. Mom took me behind the proscenium to her dressing room. It was thrilling. Our picture was taken for the local paper and she signed my script: *To Ann, Peter Pan, with love, Mary Martin, Peter*. I was so flustered I forgot my script in the dressing room and so she sent down my script and a bouquet of flowers.

The director—Mary Fluhrer Nighswander—had a little acting studio above Hicky's lunch counter. She was married to a chiropractor (my father, being a medical doctor, thought chiropractors were charlatans, and Davenport, Iowa, among its other claims to fame, is the birthplace of the chiropractic art, or "science"). But Mr. Nighswander—we called him Doc—designed our flying apparatus. It was—functional. They put a lot of Kotex in your pants because the flying apparatus cut into your thighs. And of course, I was being asked to sing at the same time. It was a bit of an ordeal because the technique wasn't fully mastered. Sometimes I'd be sort of dragged across the floor and then up.

I remember, at my sixty-fifth birthday, one of my brothers was giving a toast and said: "Can you believe she played Peter Pan?" Everyone laughed. I wasn't sure if it was a joke about my age, or my fear of flying, or my waistline—or all three. At any rate everyone laughed.

But I wasn't ever scared to fly in a theater. I loved it—it was a great excitement. It was after I had children I was afraid to fly; I'm one of those people who thinks they have to keep the plane aloft by worrying. My worry keeps so many things aloft. Or did, until the inevitable inertia crept in and so many people started dying. My husband, my mother, and now—But let's not talk about that.

My father is a great lover of roses and grew them in the backyard. He was out of the house a lot when I was little because he vaccinated, weighed, and generally took care of all the babies in town. He always carried around his brown doctor's bag, just in case. The mumps, the measles, rubella—coxsackie virus, these were the siren songs that kept him out of the house on 111 McClellan Boulevard. So there were lots of things he missed in my childhood. But he never missed me playing Peter Pan.

*The curtain parts.*

MOVEMENT ONE:
in the nursery, that is to say
the nursing home, that is to say the hospital

*Ann/1's father, George, is underneath a sheet, dying.*
*He is eighty-four and has lived a good and long life and now has*
*leukemia.*

*His sons and youngest daughter are clustered around the small room.*
*The room is spare. There is probably no window, but if there were,*
*Davenport, Iowa, would be outside, stalwart and unmoving, by the*
*moving Mississippi River.*
*There is a television in the corner, high up, the way they have in*
*hospitals.*
*And some utilitarian hospital chairs.*
*And a door into an unseen sterile corridor.*
*The low murmur of hospital beeps.*
*Wendy/5 is rubbing her father's feet.*

*1 is doing a crossword puzzle.*
*John/2, Jim/3, and Michael/4 are alternately adjusting their*
*father's hospital lines and blankets.*
*A keeping watch, a long vigil, together. A short silence.*
*Then:*

1

What's a five-letter word for a public square in Greece?

2

Piazza.

4

That would be six letters and Italian.

2

Well I was close. Pizza—

3

—is five letters. And food.

2

Anyone hungry?

1

Agora! Yes!
I wonder if that's related to agonal breathing—

3

*(Correcting the pronunciation)* agonal—

1

Oh, in rhetorical theory it's agonal—

3

Well, in medicine it's agonal.

5

Can you pass me the lotion?

1

I wonder what the etymology is—agon—struggle—

4

Maybe it's agony for people to meet in a public square.

1

Isn't it the heart of our democracy?

3

Democracy is agony. At least, at the present moment—when the White House is occupied by Slick Willy—

1

Must we refer to our president as Slick Willy?

5

Let's not start—

1

Eight down—To move laterally . . . eight letters—anyone?

4

Sidle—no—that's five—

3

Slither—no seven—they always like those overly clever puns— maybe something football related—like a lateral pass—speaking of, is the Notre Dame game on?

4

Think so.

2

I don't think so, I know so.

3

Anyone mind?

*They shake their heads.*

4

Dad would probably want to hear it.

*3 turns the television on.*

5

Could you mute it?

*He mutes it.*

1

Shuffle? No—

4

How many letters again?

1

Eight.

4

A medical term? Lateral meniscus—no—

1

Sidestep! Last week I finally finished a *New York Times* Sunday crossword puzzle all by myself. Probably because it was easy.

5

Don't diminish yourself.

1

No I'm really not very good at them.

2

*(To 1)* We all know you got the highest SAT scores, Annie—
You don't need to be self-deprecating—

4

I think they're tattooed on your arm somewhere—see right there—

1

Oh stop it—

3

And now that you have your PhD in—what is it?

1

Rhetoric—

3

Rhetoric, right—Now you'll be indomitable—

5

Now I'm the only one in the family who's not a doctor—

2

I'm not a doctor.

5

But you teach at a college—don't they call you professor?

2

Sometimes.

1

Anyway, I had a lot of answers for free because it was about the Beatles—

3

*(Overlapping)* "Can't buy me love ... love ..."

ALL

"Can't buy me lo–ove–huuuuuuuuhhhhh ..."

5

Remember how you boys had that bus and you called the "buh" and you would play the Beatles and drive around and pick up girls on the bus? I would never have gotten away with that. Mom and Dad had such a double standard for girls.

2

Oh I think you got away with plenty.

3

*(About the football game)* What quarter is it?

2

Fourth.

1

Remember how nervous Dad used to get at Jim's football games? He was like a maniac, chewing gum and pacing the sidelines—

3

Yeah.


4

He never came to my games.


2

Well you weren't All American—


*A surprising play on the football game on television. The men groan.*


4

Well, we all know I wasn't terribly athletic. I did however get to go to the state championship one year in golf and Dad said: "I'm not coming. Whenever I watch you play you play badly and I want you to play well."


1

So he didn't come?


4

No.


5

That's terrible.


1

Did you play well?


4

I was heroic.

*2 laughs.*
*A groan from George.*

1

Dad?

4

I'll get the doctor.

3

I'll go.

*3 gets up and exits for a moment.*
*They all hold their father.*
*3 comes back.*

4

What'd he say?

3

Dad's regular doctor is on vacation. The guy covering said: "The order's written for morphine PRN."

5

What does that mean?

3

He said: "If your dad is in pain, we can up the dosage of morphine. Otherwise, we'll just have to wait. I understand your situation, I went through this with my own family. But there are euthanasia laws in the state of Iowa. And this is a Catholic hospital."

4

What an asshole.

1

What is he accusing us of?

4

Of being less than Catholic because we asked for morphine.

1

I hate this.

2

We all hate this.

3

I can't believe I've practiced medicine for thirty years only to be
to reduced to one bureaucratic order written by an out-of-town
doctor while my father is dying.

5

So what does that mean, practically speaking?

3

It means we say he's in pain every hour and the nurse will up the
dosage.

5

Isn't that sort of—like—

4

What?

1

You know—

4

No—

1

Like we're killing him?

### 3

No, we're giving palliative care which this hospital is too screwed up to do.

### 1

My rational sense tells me it's okay, the morphine, but emotionally—

### 4

Annie—

### 1

*(To 3 and 4)* You both know better than I do, being doctors—and in some ways it's worse for you—having to handle the medical side of things—when it's your own father—but it just doesn't seem—right—

### 3

He's in pain, Annie.

### 2

Now look, Annie, I've been taking care of Dad for the last two years, and I know when he's in pain. He's in a lot of pain right now. He would want us to help him.

### 4

He's not walking out of here, Annie. I'm sorry.

*1 starts crying.*

### 5

I'm with Ann. What's your rush? He'll let go when he's ready.

### 3

It's not about rushing, my God. It's about staying ahead of the pain.

1

It just—it reminds me of when we put the dog down—her body was riddled with cancer—she couldn't walk, bleeding on the floor, it seemed like the right thing to do—but in the moment— at the vet—she sort of woke up—came to herself—she had these bright eyes—I was holding her paw—then this sterile injection— she looked up at me with these big eyes—like forgive them they know not what they do—and I felt like I killed her—I don't want to kill Dad!

*1 cries.*
*2 puts his arm around her.*

4

We can hold off on the morphine for now. If it makes you uncomfortable.

1

Well yes I guess it does. Thanks.

*They sit.*
*They wait.*
*1 eats a mint.*

1

Mint?

*She offers.*
*No one takes one.*
*The sound of 1 eating a mint.*
*Hospital machines beep.*
*The doctors—3 and 4—adjust George's lines and look at his numbers;*
*4 takes his pulse.*

3

What's his pulse?

4

Still forty.

1

Is that good?

3

Not really. Blood pressure?

4

Sixty over thirty.

1

Which is—

3

Not good.
But he doesn't want to go.
He's strong. He doesn't want to quit.
Oh, Dad.

4

On one hand you want this damn thing over with and on the other hand you'd give your life for one more day. Jesus Christ.

*A pause.*

1

Should someone go out and get food?

5

I'm not hungry.
I don't want to leave.
I think I have a bagel from the airport if anyone wants it—

*She produces a bagel from her purse.*
*They all shake their heads.*
*The light outside changes from afternoon to evening light.*
*3 walks to the window, watching the light change.*
*4 falls asleep.*
*2 sits by his father.*
*1 falls asleep.*
*5 stays up.*
*An ambulance siren in the distance.*

2

What *time* is it—

3

God only knows . . .

*George appears to wake with an unbearable rattle in his throat.*

1

*(Waking)* What's that?

3

*(To 4)* Do you have the suction?

*4 hands it to 3.*
*3 suctions the excess fluid from his father's throat.*

3

*(To 4)* Towel.

5

Is this it?

3

Hard to say. Could be.

*5 sings; she has a beautiful voice:*

5

"The water is wide, but I can't cross over..."

1

That's so pretty, did we sing that at your wedding, it's such a sad song to sing at a wedding ... *(She looks at her father)* He looks like a—a—what are those portraits—divided into dark and light—those Rembrandt self-portraits doesn't he ... sort of yellow....

5

*(To 1)* Do you have to intellectualize everything?

1

Sorry, am I?

*Agonal breathing from their father.*

2

Dad, do you want us to help you to go, Dad?

4

We're going to berryland, Dad, berryland—

1

What's he talking about, walleye fishing?

4

It's a place I went with Dad—just me and him—near the four-
teenth hole at sunset—you could eat berries there—we called it
berryland—

*4 holds his father.*

2

*(Quiet)* Dad, Dad, 15-2, 15-4, 15-6, 15-8.

*1 looks mystified.*

2

*(To 1)* Cribbage scores.

2

Do you know we love you, Dad?

*They hold him.*
*The machines go back to regular pulses.*

5

Every time we touch him he comes back. It's as though no one
ever touched him before. He's so happy to be touched.

1

I'm sure Mom never touched his feet. His feet probably haven't
been touched in years.

3

Maybe never.

1

Maybe never.

2

It's okay for you to go, Dad. You gave us each other.

1

What do those numbers mean?

3

His heart rate is stable again.

5

Oh my God.

2

*(To 5)* You should get some sleep. We all should.

*A silence.*
*They all go to sleep in their chairs.*
*A glimmer of morning light.*
*Someone is sleeping on the remote control and shifts their weight.*
*The television goes on by accident to loud static and then an insipid*
*commercial comes on.*

VOICEOVER FROM THE TV

Pilates. For a younger and more beautiful you. You can go from
flab to fit with as little as twenty minutes a day. Pilates instruc-
tors pay up to $1,200 for a professional Pilates chair. But you'll pay
only $14.95. That's right $14.95.

4

*(Overlapping with "younger")* What?

1

What time is it?

3

Morning. We got through the night.


4

How are his vitals?


3

Let me see.


VOICEOVER FROM THE TV

Pilates. It's a fitness revolution. And you don't even have to leave your home . . . your body longer, leaner, sexier . . . But you have to act now. Come on, get off the couch and get onto the chair. This special offer is not available in stores. Call this toll free number . . .


2

*(Overlapping with "Pilates")* Mike's been doing Pilates.


3

Why doesn't he look beautiful then?


5

He does. He does look beautiful.


1

Will someone please turn that off?

*4 flicks the remote to turn on the VCR.*
*It is now their home movies from childhood.*
*They all react. There is no dialogue—the movies were silent—but we*
*hear a Benny Goodman or Glenn Miller version of "And the Angels*
*Sing."*

5

Oh!

2

Look how skinny we are! Annie, look how skinny you are!

1

*(To 2)* Look how skinny you are!

5

*(To 4)* Did you put this together?

4

Yeah. I converted all the home movies to VHS. For Dad.

1

Oh, that's so nice! You're the nicest one of us. You really are.

5

I didn't know it was a competition.

2

Did you add the music?

4

Yeah, they give you the option to add a song, so I put in Mom and Dad's song.

1

Aw . . .

2

*(Referring to the home movie)* There you are dancing, Wendy. You were always dancing.

4

You were the apple of Dad's eye.
There we are—all coming downstairs on Christmas morning.


1

Oh my God it looks so staged.


5

We had to go in order—oldest first—me last—


3

I was always at the vanishing point in all the pictures—


5

I always thought it was my role to be invisible—


3

Seriously?


4

You were the caboose who got all the attention—


3

I don't mean vanishing as in invisible—


1

He means vanishing as in most important—


3

I was in the middle—with two on either side—technically that's
the vanishing point—as the middle child you're supposed to be
all screwed up but I was just slightly taller—


2

What? Were not.

*Then a red-headed teenage girl comes on the invisible screen as*
*Peter Pan.*

4

Annie, look—it's you—as Peter Pan!

3

My God, Ann, look at you.

4

Dad was so proud of your being Peter Pan. But I remember when
you did that avant-garde stuff in Chicago and Dad just couldn't
understand why you had to say damn when you could have said
darn.

1

There I am, arms akimbo. *(She crows)*

3

I think you're about to fly! Annie when I was little I thought
flying was real because I watched you fly in *Peter Pan*. So now
when I fly in my dreams I'm somehow always flying in *Peter Pan*.
And it couldn't be more real. Oh—there you go! You're flying!

*They all look at her flying for a while.*
*She watches herself flying on television.*
*Suddenly, the beeping of hospital monitors.*
*Confusion.*
*Then the hospital television channel changes from home movies to*
*fuzz.*
*George looks up as though he sees something.*
*He desperately grabs at his hospital gown.*
*His kids rush to him.*

1

What's happening? Dad?

3

This is it.

5

Look to the light!

2

Dad?

1

Dad!

3

We're here—

*4 weeps.*
*George dies.*
*2 and 4 take his medical tubing off of him.*
*1 begins to say the Lord's Prayer.*
*The others join.*

1

Our Father, who art in Heaven,

ALL

Hallowed be thy name . . .
Thy Kingdom come,
Thy will be done—
On Earth as it is in Heaven.
Give us this day our daily bread,
And forgive us our trespasses,

As we forgive those who trespass against us;
And lead us not into temptation,
But deliver us from evil.
Amen.

*A small sound: ping.*
*The lights change.*
*George very simply gets up from his hospital bed.*
*His children don't see him.*
*They continue to look down at the hospital bed as though he is there.*
*And George leaves.*
*The siblings, now without parents, stand with their arms around*
*each other.*
*3 begins singing softly:*

3

Oh when the saints
Oh when the saints

ALL

Oh when the saints
Oh when the saints go marching in
Lord I want to be in that number
When the saints go marching in . . .

*If they play instruments, they might now form a ragtag five-piece*
*band with trumpet and accordion and sing and play "When the*
*Saints Go Marching In."*
*Or a marching band might enter.*
*Or they might just sing the song, with some homespun attempts at*
*harmony.*
*And push the hospital bed off, ceremonially.*

MOVEMENT TWO:
the Irish wake

*The idea of a breakfast nook.*
*A small breakfast table, wooden and round with drop leaves and*
*rolling feet, appears, and a hanging lamp appears over it.*
*A door leads to an unseen kitchen.*
*And they all sit around their old breakfast nook and tell jokes and*
*philosophize and fight about politics and drink whiskey and eat*
*Chex party mix out of a big red tin.*
*The night before the funeral.*
*Someone has just told a joke. They are all laughing at it.*
*3 is pouring whiskey.*

4

Let's have another.

3

What's an Irish wake without Jameson's—

*3 pours whiskey into 1's, then 2's, then his own glass.*

1

A wake should have a body shouldn't it—so weird to leave the
hospital—to leave the body—
Like we were abandoning him . . .

5

Without a ritual . . .

1

Yes—

*3 pours into 4's glass.*

4

I meant let's have another joke—but I'll keep the whiskey, thank
you very much.

2

Anyone got another joke?

*4, the joke teller, is an internist. 3 is a surgeon. So 4 tells the joke
pointedly to 3.*

4

I do. An internist dies and goes to Heaven (as you would expect
after a lifetime of selfless service to mankind) . . .

3

Yeah, yeah—

4

Anyway, St. Peter is taking him on an orientation tour, showing him the golf course, the fitness center—

2

Is there a hot tub?

4

Absolutely. Anyway, it's time for lunch so they go to the heavenly cafeteria and stand in a long line. Soon, a man with a long flowing beard, wearing scrubs and surgical clogs, with a stethoscope around his neck, comes in and goes right to the front of the line. The internist asks St. Peter, "Who the hell is that guy?" St. Peter responds, "Oh, that's God, he just thinks he's a surgeon."

*Some laugh.*
*Some groan.*
*3 cheers.*

3

That's right! To God!

2

You tell one, Ann—

1

I can never remember jokes. Is that a woman thing?

3

Yes. Just kidding.

1

*(With irony)* Hilarious.
Maybe I never learned jokes because I didn't go to medical school.

4

*(To 3)* It's true. We did learn jokes in medical school.

1

No one really tells jokes anymore. They tell sort of—ironic stories with no punch lines. Do you think that's less democratic—that stand-up comedians have sort of ironic *personas*—but no jokes you can retell—

3

I don't think it's about irony, it's about *political correctness*, you can't offend anyone—

1

Oh please let's not say political correctness tonight—

5

It's better to offend people?

3

No really, we've become humorless—

2

How many feminists does it take to change a light bulb?

2, 3, 4, AND 1

That's not funny!

1

Okay, okay, *enough. Anyway*—I can only remember one joke.

2

Tell it!

1

*(Dramatic)* So—this carrot was crossing the road. True story. And he gets run over by a truck and he's bleeding in the road, and there's carrot blood everywhere—

2

*(Overlapping and chuckling)* Carrot blood—

1

—and his friend takes him to the doctor and the doctor comes out of surgery, pulls his mask down, and says, "I have some good news and some bad news," and the friend says, "Oh doctor, please tell me the good news first." "All right. Your friend is going to live." "Oh, thank God, thank God, doctor. What's the bad news?" "Well, I'm afraid he's going to remain a vegetable for the rest of his life."

*Some laugh, some groan.*

| 2 | 3 |
|---|---|
| Oh God. | Jesus. |

1

That was Pat's favorite joke.

5

Aw, Pat.

4

Pat did love the puns.

1

Who was it who said that puns are the lowest form of humor?

2

It wasn't your husband, I can tell you that.
To Pat.

ALL

To Pat.

*They all raise a glass.*
*They drink.*

2

To Dad.

ALL

To Dad.

*They raise a glass again.*
*A slight pause—a hole in time.*
*George comes in, wearing a cardigan sweater, a dress shirt, and*
*nice brown trousers. He wears glasses. He has a kind face.*
*He is an ordinary ghost.*
*He has returned home and is going about his business.*
*He reads a newspaper at the table. The* Des Moines Register.
*They don't see him. He doesn't pay much attention to them.*
*They drink.*

5

To Mom.

ALL

To Mother.

4

Maybe they're all up there together.

1

Mom and Dad? Fighting?

4

They only fought when they drank Wild Turkey. No drinking in Heaven.

1

It's funny but when Mom died I remember being so relieved when Dad and I were buying her casket; I wasn't relieved she was dead, I was relieved she wasn't there to argue with Dad about what kind of casket to buy. With me stuck in between them.

5

That's terrible.

4

It seems so dark—a casket—so cold . . .

1

Mmm.

*George leaves the room and goes to the toilet.*

4

When John and I went to pick out Dad's coffin this afternoon we saw Bobby McCabe—

ALL

Bobby McCabe!

4

—Who said, "Now, you've got the five-thousand-dollar one here and the ten-thousand-dollar one there." I said, "What do you get for the extra five grand?" He said, "You get a better seal and the degeneration is slower" . . . And I said, "Isn't that sort of the point? To degenerate?" He said in this pointed way: *"Some people just feel better spending more money."* I said let's get the cheap casket. And for the first time cremation made sense.

2

Dad is much too much a Catholic to get cremated.

*The toilet flushes.*

2

That toilet never stops running. I'll go.

*2 exits to fix the toilet.*
*George comes back.*
*They pass each other, unseeing.*

4

I don't think Dad was absolute about Catholicism. I remember when I went to Sacred Heart the nuns told us if one member of the family became a priest the whole family was saved so in third grade I thought: I'll take one for the team, and I said: I want to be a priest.

*2 comes back, having jiggled the toilet handle.*

3

Wow.

4

Then Sister Mary Bethel pulls Dad aside at a parent teacher conference and says: "We think Mikey has received *the call*," and Dad said: "Well, is that right?" The next week, I was in public school.

2

Hank Lischer was recruiting me for public school. He said the desks were automatic and the inkwells came up by themselves.

4

It's true, I'm sorry you didn't get to experience that.

*They all laugh.*

3

All I know is Sister Mary Robert Cecile—

4

We called her Big Bob—

| 1 | 5 |
|---|---|
| Big Bob!! | Big Bob? |

3

Big Bob!—whacked me with a ruler in front of the class for trying to look up her dress, a feat the Lord himself could not accomplish.

2

Nor would He want to.

3

Nor would He want to.

5

Maybe I ended up having the most interest in religion because I never went to Catholic school. I used to shut myself in my room for days of solitary contemplation. Dad and I used to go to Mass every week during Lent. You were all grown up and out of the house.

1

Would Mom go with you to Mass?

4

No, Mom was a Lutheran atheist to the bitter end. She said: "I never understood how there could be a Heaven. It would be too heavy and all the bodies would fall down."

5

She used to say: "Man created God as a means of social control. Religion teaches you not to think."

1

Well, I guess I associate religion with stupidity too.

4

Jesus, Ann.

1

Sorry. Well, the religious right anyway.

2

Liberals make the mistake of conflating religion with ignorance, it's an ethical and a tactical error—

5

Could we please not say "liberal" or "conservative" tonight? I'm not in the mood, I'm really not.

2

Sorry.

3

Here, have some Jameson's, you'll feel better.

5

No thanks. I'm going to get some water. Would anyone else like water?

| 1 | 2 | 3 |
|---|---|---|
| No thanks. | Nah. | Uh-uh. |

*5 gets up and goes offstage to get some water.*
*George follows her.*

2

Ann, when did you stop going to church?

1

I was taking the pill after I gave birth to Katherine, and I was going to Mass at St. Clement's where she was baptized and I thought, Well, I'm taking birth control so I'm in mortal sin, and it's hypocritical for me to go to church, I should stay home and read the *New York Times* instead—

2

Ah, yes the great church of the *New York Times*—

1

All right—

4

Annie I remember you as quite the Catholic. We would all be in the basement during a tornado and you were maybe twelve years old leading the Act of Contrition and of course a few Hail Marys thrown in—

1

I probably liked the drama of it.

*5 comes back in with water.*
*She drinks it.*

1

I loved all the drama—the May altars—
*oh Mary we crown thee with blossoms today, queen of the angels,*
*queen of the May— (They all chime in singing too)*
And the mournful advent songs—Midnight Mass—everything
about Christmas—

2

Remember the year of the lutefisk?

3

Oh God the lutefisk.

*They all laugh.*

4

Mother decided to get in touch with her Scandinavian roots—

1

Oh it was awful!

4

The smell—

3

An affront to the olfactory nerves—

1

The texture!

4

Gelatinous gobs of herring—

5

Preserved in lye—

1

Lye, can you imagine!

2

But we were really uncharitable—no one would eat it—Mother
was reduced to tears—

3

We were pretty merciless—

5

You were.

1

One year Mom and I shopped for dresses for the Christmas dance
and we found two we both liked and—if you can imagine—I had
a hard time choosing.

2, 3, 4, AND 5

*(Overlapping, with irony)* What/No!/Impossible/Not you, Annie!

1

Anyway, I finally chose one—it was blue chiffon. And then on
Christmas morning my other dress was there—green satin.

5

Oh! The green satin—

1

With the square neck, square back, and big bow in the back. It
was such a surprise.

2

Remember the Santa paper?

1

Mom would be wrapping and smoking all night—

4

Amazing she didn't burn the house down—

2

And one year she ran out of Santa paper in the middle of the night—it was an emergency—she was so worried Wendy would realize—

5

Aw, Mom.

3

Remember Otto Stegmaier? *(They echo "Otto Stegmaier")* When I was eight, he made an off-the-cuff comment about Santa Claus being a phony. And he turned to me and asked me if I still believed in him. Honestly I'd never given it a moment's thought. I said, "Nah, I don't believe in him." The tone of his question left only one possible answer. I sort of succumbed to the tone and believed the answer. And I think I got that one right . . .

*He drinks.*

5

Well, I think that's sad. I think Santa Claus is real.

3

What?

5

In a way.

1

Do you mean that there is a word, Santa Claus, an idea Santa Claus, that is real, so therefore Santa Claus is real?

4

That's like saying unicorns are real because there is a word and a mental picture for them.

*George comes back in with a Santa Claus hat on.*
*He holds a grapefruit and a grapefruit spoon.*
*He puts fake sugar on his grapefruit and eats it.*

1

That's an old problem in linguistics—

5

I wasn't really thinking of linguistics, I mean that during Christmas time—we *choose* to give—so the spirit of Santa Claus—exists.

4

That's very "yes Virginia there is a Santa Claus" of you.

1

I suppose, in that sense, Santa Claus-ing, the action of being Santa Claus, exists, it just doesn't match the picture of a unified Santa Claus.

5

I'm not sure what you just said, Ann. But I think that when we pray we make God happen.

*The boys all drink.*
*George squeezes his grapefruit juice into a bowl and drinks it.*
*He exits to make instant oatmeal.*

5

Do any of you pray?

*They all shake their heads.*

5

None of you? Mike?

4

Sort of. Not really. I believe in a higher power but I can't tell if it's God on my shoulder or Mom and Dad.

5

John?

2

I have conversations with God, I don't know if I'd call it praying. I remember walking around campus in the winter of my junior year with the Jesuits and I wrote down everything I thought I'd ever done wrong in my life and then I tore up the pieces of paper as small as I could so no one would ever recognize the handwriting and threw them into the wind and I said: No more. No more guilt.

4

I never knew that.

2

Yeah, well.

3

That's deep.

2

*(To 3)* All right, shut up. What about you? You must have prayed when you were a quarterback.

3

I prayed so much as a young soldier of Christ it lost all meaning. Annie I couldn't believe it when you broke into the Our Father when we were holding vigil over Dad. Okay, he was "our father" and it was an appropriate choice, but you've been railing for decades against the bullshit in the Catholic Church. Maybe you haven't strayed so far from the flock.

1

I still take communion to be sociable. I do miss it, the affiliation but—

3

But—

1

I just can't—I don't have an explanation for the world. I don't have an explanation for what happens after death.

5

Doesn't that make you afraid of dying?

1

Yes. Of course I'm afraid of dying. It's organized my entire life. Aren't you afraid of dying?

5

No. I think it's like changing clothes. I think the moment will be beautiful. Liberating. I think I've done it before. I think I've had lots of lives.

1

Oh.

4

Hm.

1

I wish I could believe that. It sounds nice.

*George enters, not in his Santa Claus hat anymore.*
*He eats some Chex party mix.*
*They don't notice.*

4

Annie, I wish I could prove to you that consciousness persists. I think you'd be less afraid.

1

How could you?

4

Dad—if you're here with us, give us a sign.

*A silence.*
*George drops the bowl of Chex party mix on the floor.*
*A hubbub. They all react with surprise, overlapping:*

1

Oh my God—

2

Holy shit!

5

I told you!

*George exits.*

2

Well, I have no fear of death. I spend no time thinking of it. If there's life after death, wonderful. If there isn't, what's the point of worrying. Can't do anything about it.

3

You don't think you're in denial?

2

No. Life is for the living.

5

That's what Mom always said.

4

Well, I'm afraid of dying. I think there's a scientific part of me that wonders: What is it like to die? And I sort of assume my mind would survive that experience. I'm going to miss a whole lot of people. I think the scary thing is not knowing if they're going to miss me. I remember when we had to put down Capp, I thought: What is the meaning of the life of a dog? I hope when I die people remember me more than they would remember the family dog . . . on the other hand it's not a competition so if they want to remember Capp more than me that's fine too . . .

*George reenters with the old family dog.*
*They don't see it.*
*The dog eats the Chex party mix off the floor.*
*George pats the dog.*

1

I guess I live so much in my own consciousness that the idea of not being here—of that ceasing . . . is terrible . . . Then I apply logic and say: but I won't know—so . . . But I would like my consciousness to persist so I can see my grandchildren grow up. I'd like to see their graduations, their . . .

2

Of course.

1

. . . growing up.

3

But what does it mean to be a grown-up?

4

All I know is my mantra used to be: immortality through immaturity!

3

Do you feel like a grown-up, Annie?

1

No. When I think of grown-ups I think of Dad wearing that hat—
*(Gesturing to a hat hanging on the wall)* —a grown-up man's hat—
to work every day—not because it kept you warm but because that's what grown-ups did. I pride myself somehow on—not feeling grown up.

2

So you only have bad associations with growing up—

1

Growing up means—planning. Even though I like plans and lists I've never had *A Plan*.

2

Well by that definition isn't being a grown-up a good thing? Someone who plans?

1

Maybe. I can't seem to shake the disappointment that I haven't— done something—whatever that would be. Dad always said: "I never praised you kids because I didn't want you to get swelled heads."

2

He was not free with the compliments. It was always:

2, 3, AND 4

"He who flatters me does me an injustice."

1

One time Dad said to me driving home from an Iowa football game: "Well you're very smart, Annie." But it made me feel like he was saying: "You're smart so why have you not accomplished anything?"

5

Geez.

2

Of course Dad was proud of you.

1

He used to say, "You're so smart, Annie, you shouldn't be a teacher. You could have been a lawyer."

3

Well, yeah . . .

1

And that's what I associate with being grown up—programmed—ossified—I remember my deep almost primitive hatred of Nixon and wondering if it wasn't somehow to do with Dad . . .

3

Do you remember having to be in the children's brigade for Nixon?

1

I was out of the house by then, thank God—

3

Kennedy came through town that election cycle and was motorcading on River Drive. I was holding a Nixon sign assuring balance to the proceedings. He came by in an open convertible, in the back seat, just like in Dallas. Everyone cheering. My eyes zeroed in on him and I started running after the motorcade. He was the enemy in my mind, just as the Ohio State football team was the enemy of the Hawkeyes, my team. I was madly yelling obscenities and booing him; but all the while I had him in my eye and couldn't stop thinking how cool he was and wondering why in the hell I was doing what I was doing. And secretly inside I joined the cheering. How could I not . . .

4

I wonder if the whole country grew up after JFK was shot.

2

Either that or the whole country decided never to grow up after JFK was shot.

1

*(To 2)* Do you feel like a grown-up?

2

Yeah and I'm tired of it.

1

When did you feel like a grown-up?

2

When I got a seat at the big table.

1

What?

2

You know the big dining room table rather than the little kid card table at holidays?

1

Wow that's so literal. Michael?

4

As the fourth of five I had the luxury of never having to grow up; I was always little Mikey as soon as I crossed the threshold. I defer to everyone, I don't know why Wendy doesn't defer to me. *(5 rolls her eyes)*

No, but seriously I think I grew up during my medical training. When they first called a code I would run in the other direction but by the end of my residency I ran *toward* the code. And that felt sort of grown up.

1

Wendy?

5

As a child I thought growing up was getting married, and I never wanted to do that because married people looked so bored with each other and I never wanted to be like that. I wanted to run into fountains with my clothes on.

1

And when you got married?

5

Yes—but not overnight—it was finding a livelihood where I could help other people. It was learning to get out of the way.

3

*(To 1)* So you're the only one who doesn't feel like a grown-up?

1

I guess.

3

Well, if you don't grow up you don't have to die.
Here's to not growing up, Annie. You and me!

1

Here's to not growing up.

*3 and 1 clink glasses.*

4

You can grow up before you die or not grow up before you die, but either way you're going to die. Give me some of that.

*More liquor is poured into everyone's cup.*
*5 holds her hand up, refusing more whiskey.*

1

And dying is such a failure.

3

How do you mean?

1

Our bodies are the enemy and dying is a capitulation to a foreign shore.

3

Do you experience your body as the enemy?

1

*(To 3)* Don't you?

3

No.

1

You cut cancer out of people's bodies. Aren't you sort of the hero and the body is this enemy?

3

Cancer is the enemy. You're marshaling the body's resources. The body is your closest ally.

2

Like Canada?

ALL

*(Standing and singing the first line of the anthem)* O, Canada!

1

I'd like it if Canada were Heaven—I'd go to the Shaw festival—

*They laugh.*
*A pause.*

3

I remember once driving into Manhattan on an August Sunday to see a patient. The day was hot as hell, nobody on the street. It was so still, like everyone was at a party elsewhere and I was the only one not invited. I thought: Is this what death is like? Awful.

1

It's funny, I think I believe in Tinker Bell more than I do in the afterlife. I stopped believing in God when I noticed that all the myths were the same— I was teaching the myth of Prometheus and suddenly I thought—Prometheus—oh! He's just like Jesus! And I thought about Greek myths and how silly they seem to us now and how our myths will seem just as silly to those who come after us—

5

But if they're all the same metaphor I mean doesn't that prove something?

*George reenters with orange juice and some Metamucil.*

1

*(As in, she's interested and thinks it's a good point)* Hmm.

4

A good Catholic doesn't think God is a metaphor.
When the little bell rings it's real.

2

I should know, I was an altar boy. I rang that bell.

1

Like Tinker Bell.

*George stirs the Metamucil with his spoon and it makes a little tinkling sound. They look up for a moment, registering the sound, then dismiss it.*

3

Well I think it's all a metaphor.

5

But metaphors are real that's what I'm trying to say—

1

Anyway, isn't it weird that I *religiously* believe fairies onstage are real; it isn't a very useful belief... but I don't believe in an afterlife even though it could be a useful belief.

2

But you can't just choose your whole belief system based on usefulness, can you?

3

There are consequences to having a false belief.

1

Well sure—

2

5

Take this country for example.     No thanks.
We've confused self-interest
with selfishness.

4

We have! No one really understands anything about economics; of course I understand everything about economics . . . *(A self-deprecating laugh)*

3

You know what's really wrong with this country? Too many crazed and half-witted Platonists and too few sensible Aristotelians who want to roll up their sleeves and get things done.

1

I suppose you think liberals are the crazed, half-witted Platonists?

3

I don't even know if Plato was a Platonist . . . .

4

Now you've lost me.

3

Plato goes like this *(Pointing up)* and Aristotle goes like that. *(Pointing down)* Liberals believe in unreal worlds—Neverland if you will—and conservatives are pragmatists who try to solve problems on the ground.

1

*(With irony)* Newt Gingrich being a paragon of practical wisdom?

5

Do we have to fight about politics tonight?

3

Dad would have approved.

4

Then let's fight!

2

You know what Dad used to say—if you're not a liberal before the age of twenty you have no heart and if you're not conservative after the age of forty you have no brain— *(3 and 4 echo "have no brain")*

1

The idea of conservatives being the grown-up party is absurd— the party of Lincoln used to be pragmatic, now you're all insane—

*George finishes his drink and exits to the kitchen.*

3

How would you know, you don't read conservative papers, we read the *New York Times* every day but when's the last time you've picked up a conservative paper—or read William Safire— or Ann Coulter—

*1 screams.*

2

Oh ho!

1

I wouldn't dream of reading Ann Coulter—she's an idiot witch—

4

How do you know if she's an idiot if you don't read her—

3

She's not exactly my first choice, but if she were liberal you would say she was a sassy Joan of Arc—

1

Don't you dare insult Joan of Arc—

3

Oh I forgot you played her in college—

| 4 | 1 |
|---|---|
| I read Nicholas Kristof even though I don't agree. | Good for you. |

| 2 | 1 |
|---|---|
| He advocates socialism—<br>Is a businessman really worth<br>a billion dollars? No.<br>But the gross redistribution of<br>income makes no sense either.<br>We've incentivized the wrong<br>behavior. | What???! |
| | What are you talking about?<br>The welfare state is gone.<br>Bill Clinton just dismantled<br>it. |

2

The welfare state is far from gone! It is alive and well and ever-expanding!

1

Dad lived through the Depression. *He ate squirrels.* He shot squirrels and *ate* them because he was hungry. Why was he so undone by the concept of the have-nots being helped?

4

Dad did pro bono work all the time and never asked for recognition—

3

Dad grew up dirt poor. His father was educated, was even a lawyer, but he was a small-town lawyer in a town that was too small to need one.

1

Exactly—how can people who have struggled so much in the past lose all empathy for people who struggle in the present?

3

Let me finish. Dad didn't even have a bathroom in his house. When he moved into a house with five functioning toilets—

2

*(Overlapping)* Almost functioning—

3

—almost, can you imagine how flushed (sorry) he felt with success? *(Some groan, some laugh)* He went to a subsidized state university on the GI Bill—

1

*(Overlapping)* Exactly my point—

3

—but it wasn't enough. He waited on tables at the student union. He met Mom because he waited on her.

ALL

*(With nostalgia and repeated family storytelling ritual)* Made her a hamburger in the shape of a heart. Poured on ketchup for blood.

3

He won her over! In his mind he pulled himself out of the prairie, out of the Depression, out of the outhouse—into our house. He became somebody, he became a contender. He works his ass off to send us to good schools and we come back espousing views that undermine his life narrative. So he flicks the channel and watches another episode of *Archie Bunker*. It is his refuge, his post-Depression, post-outhouse refuge, how can we deny him that? How can we say he is wrong?

4

Hear, hear!

1

Why are you so angry?

3

I'm not angry.

2

Look, Dad hated that the whole idea of the family was being eroded. He cared about—you know—family values.

1

Christ . . .

2

Now, I come from this old-fashioned unit called the family, thank God, and it's a tragedy that fifty percent of this country doesn't have one! *(4 applauds)*

1

Where do you get your figures?

2

The government can't do the same job raising a family—

1

So the subtext is—

2

There's no subtext—

1

Come on that's code for—

2

I'm from the Midwest, I don't speak in codes, I say what I mean—

1

that single mothers are incapable of—

2                                        3
Of course I'm not—                    No!

1

You're interrupting—

3

*(To 1)* Annie, you take arguments personally—

1

They are personal—

4

We're just talking about ideas—it's all in good fun—

1

*Well it's not fun for me—*

2

And I would never say that about single mothers, you've been a single mother since Pat died, and you've done a beautiful job with your girls and you sure as hell deserve praise.

1

Well thank you.

2

You're welcome.

1

*(Upset)* It's just that if this family, who loves each other about as much as a family can, can't talk about politics in a civilized fashion, how do you expect the rest of the country to talk to each other at all?

4

I think this is a very civilized conversation—

5

This is not civilized! You've all had too much to drink—and—*no one listens anymore*—

2

I'm listening! My hearing is just going!

1

Political arguments are a sport for you boys and it's not a sport for us—everyone yells and interrupts on the talk shows so now we all yell and interrupt, it's awful—

4

No one was yelling! AHHHHHH! That's yelling.

1

When did you all go to the dark side? Was it under Reagan? You all sound like Aunt Helen!

2

Don't drag Aunt Helen into this—

3

She was a political genius—

1

We should be an example of a functional democracy!

5

This is not a functional democracy. And I am sick of pretending that it is! I used to feel bad for Mom cleaning all the time while the men talked politics—now I understand. She just wanted everyone to shut the hell up—so she could hear herself think! She could think better over the sink with the water running! It's all noise! Static. And I'm so goddamn tired of it! We're on a sinking ship, and you're fighting over the precise location of the deck chairs. The ocean is rising, the world is falling apart, and it's all bullshit— My God!

We're orphans now!

*A pause.*
*2 goes and hugs 5.*
*1 gets up from the table.*
*She turns to the audience.*

1

*(To the audience)* And for a moment I was transported back to the teeny breakfast nook at 111 McClellan. Mom and Dad still alive.

All of us around the wooden table, arguing about politics. Mom was bustling around the kitchen, the smell of bacon, Dad was putting NutraSweet on his grapefruit. Mom was on her eighth cigarette and eighteenth cup of coffee since five in the morning, she was smoking and needlepointing a pillow that said "The Best Is Yet to Come." Two radios are on and two televisions, one with a football game and one with *Crossfire*. We've been having the same political argument for the past thirty years—the lamp over the table was the same—but now there are no parents to adjudicate. We're supposed to be the grown-ups now.

We slept in our childhood beds that night.

*Music.*
*The lights change.*
*2, 3, 4, and 5 exit.*

*George enters with a trunk.*
*George and 1 look at each other for a moment.*
*George leaves.*
*1 opens the trunk.*
*1 goes through the trunk.*
*She sees vintage dresses which she holds to her.*
*One green satin dress.*
*One blue chiffon dress.*
*She remembers her mother.*
*Then she finds her old Peter Pan costume.*
*She puts on her Peter Pan costume.*
*She puts on her green hat.*
*She crows.*

## Movement Three:
## Neverland

### 1 AS PETER PAN

*(Whispering the lines to Wendy, waking her)* It's my last night in
the nursery . . .

*A painted screen flies in, the wall of the nursery with a window
cut into it.*
*The boys are sleeping in their beds.*

### 5 AS WENDY

It's my last night in the nursery you know.
Peter Pan is coming tonight.
Father says Peter Pan isn't real but I know he is.
I just know he is!
He's going to take me to—where?

PETER PAN

*(Whispering to her)* Neverland!

WENDY

Neverland!

*Peter Pan climbs in through the window with difficulty.*
*She stands with her arms akimbo.*

PETER PAN

Wendy!

WENDY

Peter Pan!

*They embrace.*

PETER PAN

The lost boys need a mother.
Are you ready to come to Neverland?

WENDY

Why isn't that awfully far away?

*She crows.*
*Tinker Bell rings her bell. A little light and bell onstage.*

WENDY

Oh, it's Tinker Bell!

PETER PAN

Tink! Tink! Now you behave yourself, Tink, and don't pull Wendy's hair!

WENDY

John! Michael! Wake up! Look it's a fairy!

4 AS MICHAEL AND 2 AS JOHN

A fairy!

PETER PAN

Time is a wasting! Let's go to Neverland!

WENDY

But how will I get there? I can't fly!

PETER PAN

Fairy dust!

*She sprinkles some fairy dust on her.*

WENDY

Oh!

PETER PAN

*(Upset)* But Wendy I lost my shadow!

*Peter Pan starts frantically looking for her shadow.*

PETER PAN

Do you have it, Wendy? I can't fly without my shadow!

*They all look around for her shadow.*

MICHAEL

Where did you lose it?

JOHN

What does it look like?

PETER PAN

Well, it's dark—

*They find it under the bed.*

WENDY

Here it is, Peter! I found it!

PETER PAN

Oh Wendy, bless you! But how will I get it back on?

*She tries to put it back on but it falls off.*

WENDY

I can sew your shadow back on.

PETER PAN

Do you have a sewing machine?

WENDY

Needle and thread!

*She produces a sewing basket.*

PETER PAN

I can do it.

WENDY

I can do it.

PETER PAN

I know how to sew.

WENDY

So do I. Mom taught me.


PETER PAN

No, Mom taught me.


WENDY

Mom taught me.
You're Peter Pan. You don't have a mother. And you don't know
how to sew.


PETER PAN

Right, I'm Peter Pan.


*Peter Pan puts arms akimbo and crows.*
*Wendy starts to sew.*


WENDY

I've been sending you letters, you know.


PETER PAN

We can't get letters in Neverland, Wendy. I don't have an address!


*She crows.*


WENDY

Now, Peter! I can't sew your shadow on while you're crowing.


*The family dog enters with medicine.*


WENDY

Nana! Give me that medicine. It's for Michael.
Here Michael, take your medicine.

*Wendy tries to give Michael the medicine.*

MICHAEL

I won't take it, I won't!

WENDY

Now, Michael, you must take your medicine. Father says so.

MICHAEL

I'm a doctor, I don't take medicine.

*Wendy shoves the medicine in his mouth.*
*The dog exits.*

WENDY

Now, Peter, sit still, stop trying to touch your shadow. Sit still and I'll do it.

*Wendy begins sewing Peter Pan's shadow on.*

WENDY

Everything has a shadow, Peter Pan. Honestly you should have gone to Jungian analysis. You would have learned that you can't experience joy without your dark side.

PETER PAN

I don't know what you just said, Wendy.

WENDY

You can live on Freud until you're forty but when you're seventy and facing death you either need religion or Carl Jung.

PETER PAN

Why can't I fly without my shadow?

JOHN

Think about it, Peter.

PETER PAN

What?

JOHN

A plane that's flying without its shadow on the ground is—

PETER PAN

Is what—

*John makes the sound of an explosion.*

JOHN

Poof—dead!

PETER PAN

Or just flying at night!

WENDY

I've sewn it on, Peter.

PETER PAN

Oh, well done! It's on again, my shadow is on again!

*She crows.*

PETER PAN

Now I can fly!

*She's not hooked into any flying apparatus.*
*She tries to fly, does a little jump.*

JOHN

That was the worst flying I ever saw, Peter.

PETER PAN

Sorry.
I'm afraid—

MICHAEL

What—*you* afraid, Peter Pan?

PETER PAN

I'm not afraid. My foot hurts.

JOHN

Then I'll fly.

*He jumps off something and falls.*

JOHN

Ouch.

MICHAEL

I'll do it.

*He jumps off something and falls.*
*They might keep doing this for a while—jumping off things and not*
*flying.*

JOHN

*(Sadly)* Oh. We're old, aren't we? We're getting too old to fly?

MICHAEL

One of my best friends just died.

WENDY

Me too.

MICHAEL

And I had to treat him.

JOHN

They're all getting old and dying. It's awful.

PETER PAN

No! Keep a positive attitude. We'll walk to Neverland.
Except my foot is killing me.
Could someone grab me a cane? How far a walk is Neverland?

*Someone hands her a cane from the trunk.*
*They walk toward Neverland.*

WENDY

Why Peter, you can't walk there!

PETER PAN

Right. Come! Just think wonderful thoughts and they'll lift you
up into the air!

*They raise their arms, trying to fly, and cannot fly.*

PETER PAN

March!

*They follow Peter Pan, walking with some labor.*
*They sing as they march. "Oh when the saints, oh when the saints,*
*oh when the saints go marching in . . . ."*
*Another painted piece of scenery is dropped down,*
*representing Neverland.*
*A sea, a volcano, a pirate ship.*

JOHN

It's Neverland!

MICHAEL AND WENDY

Neverland!

JOHN

There's the volcano!

MICHAEL

There's the *Jolly Roger*!

WENDY

It's so beautiful!

*Peter Pan sits down on a log.*
*She breathes into a paper bag.*

PETER PAN

Sometimes I get panic attacks when I first get to Neverland. Don't worry, it's nothing. Just, I hate travel. Airports, train stations, flying . . .

WENDY

Breathe, Peter, deep breaths.

*Peter Pan breathes in and out of the paper bag.*

PETER PAN

Maybe we shouldn't have come.

JOHN

The sun is out.
Let's play shadow tag.
Peter, you're it.

*They play shadow tag, stepping on each other's shadows.*
*Peter Pan tags Michael.*

PETER PAN

Gotcha, you're it Michael!

MICHAEL

Run, run, I'm it!

JOHN

Look at my top hat in the shadow!

WENDY

I'm standing on your head.

JOHN

Get off of my head.

WENDY

My shadow is so short!

JOHN

*(Raising his hat)* My shadow is so long! *(To Michael)* My shadow
is longer than your shadow!

MICHAEL

Is not!

JOHN

Is too!

WENDY

I didn't know it was a competition!

PETER PAN

When I turn around my shadow turns with me!

*They all spin.*

PETER PAN

Oh—dizzy—

ALL

Oh . . .

*They all get dizzy and fall down.*
*A cloud passes over the sun, taking away the shadows.*

PETER PAN

I can't see anyone's shadow!

WENDY

It's because of the clouds!

PETER PAN

Well we can't play if we can't see each other's shadows. Anyway, my foot hurts.

*Michael looks at her foot.*

MICHAEL

Let me look at it.

PETER PAN

It's not the diabetes, it's the gout.

MICHAEL

When you first feel a twinge, you have to take an anti-inflammatory. You have to stay ahead of the pain.

PETER PAN

I don't like taking ibuprofen, it causes bleeds.

JOHN

Where is Hook? I'll fight him! I'd love to kill a pirate! Ha! Ha!

*John plays with a sword.*

MICHAEL

Where are the lost boys?

JOHN

We are the lost boys.

PETER PAN

Wendy, you don't know how lucky you are to have had a mother.

WENDY

I miss her!

*Wendy starts to cry.*

PETER PAN

Oh, don't cry, Wendy! I can't stand it when you cry!

MICHAEL

I don't want to grow up.

*Michael starts to cry.*

JOHN

I don't want to grow up either!

WENDY

I want my mother!
I want my father!

                         MICHAEL

Me too!


                          JOHN

Me too!


               JOHN, MICHAEL, AND WENDY

We don't want to grow up!


*They all bawl but Peter Pan.*
*Peter Pan puts her hands over her ears.*


                        PETER PAN

I can't stand it! Tinker Bell!


*Tinker Bell appears.*


                        PETER PAN

Make them stop crying!


*Tinker Bell rings her bell.*


                        PETER PAN

How?
Oh!
Fairy dust!


*Peter Pan sprinkles fairy dust on them and they stop crying.*


                        PETER PAN

Well, that's a relief. Thanks, Tink.
Now, line up. According to age.
You here, you here, you here.

WENDY

Where do you go, Peter?

PETER PAN

I'm the oldest, so I go here.

WENDY

How can you be the oldest, Peter, if you don't grow up?

*They all line up.*

PETER PAN

I'm the oldest because I am the oldest.

*They stand in their line.*

JOHN

Now what?

WENDY

Happy birthday, Peter Pan.

PETER PAN

Is it my birthday?

ALL BUT PETER PAN

*(Chanting)* Are you one are you two are you three are you four?

PETER PAN

I don't know.
I'm quite young though.
How old am I?

JOHN

Seventy, I think!

PETER PAN

No! That can't be right! This is Neverland!

WENDY

Happy birthday, Peter Pan.

PETER PAN

What?
Is it my birthday *again*?

MICHAEL

Oh yes, time moves very fast or not at all in Neverland!

ALL BUT PETER PAN

Are you one are you two are you three are you four?—

PETER PAN

Stop it!

WENDY

Happy birthday, Peter Pan!

PETER PAN

Enough!

ALL BUT PETER PAN

Are you one are you two are you three are you four—
Are you seventy-four! Yes!

PETER PAN

No!!

*She looks at her hands.*

PETER PAN

My hands look old! Oh, dear. Oh, never mind.

*She crows.*
*Hook appears, played by 3.*

3 AS HOOK

Ah, if it isn't Peter Pan!

*Peter Pan stands up.*

PETER PAN

In the flesh, Hook! Ticktock ticktock where's your arm, Hook?

HOOK

Heard a rumor you walked here, Pan. Why didn't you fly?

PETER PAN

You must be mistaken. I flew.

HOOK

No, Peter Pan. You thought you'd never grow up. But you have.
You walked here. Slowly.
Are you ready to face me?

WENDY

*(Running up to Hook and punching him)* You big bully!

HOOK

Time for you to walk the plank little girl.

*He grabs her.*
*She bravely walks the plank, which might be a trunk or hospital*
*bed or the floor.*

PETER PAN

You won't kill my sister!
Everyone, it's time to kill Captain Hook.
Hook is death! Kill death! Make death die!

HOOK

En garde!

*Peter Pan draws her sword.*
*They duel.*

HOOK

Who are you?

PETER PAN

"I am youth! I am joy!"

HOOK

Then fly!

*They duel.*
*Hook suddenly has his sword to her neck.*

PETER PAN

I want my mother.

WENDY

Oh, Peter!

PETER PAN

"Cowards die many times before their deaths / The valiant never
taste of death but once!"

*Peter Pan closes her eyes, brave.*
*Hook kills Peter Pan.*

HOOK

Finally!

*Peter Pan sits back up.*

PETER PAN

Oh! "Death will be an awfully big adventure!"

HOOK

*(Whining)* "I'll never grow up, never grow up," that'll teach you, Pan.

*John, Michael, and Wendy fall upon Peter Pan's body and cry.*
*Secretly, they are attaching Peter Pan to flying cables.*
*Tinker Bell appears.*
*Tinker Bell rings and rings, trying to get Wendy's attention.*

WENDY

What are you saying, Tink?
Oh!

*Wendy approaches the audience.*

WENDY

She says, if you believe in Peter Pan, clap, please clap! Do you believe in Peter Pan?

*The audience claps.*

WENDY

Oh thank you, oh thank you!

*Peter Pan comes back to life and is hoisted into the air.*

PETER PAN

Oh!
Oh!
I'm flying!
I'm flying!
Hook, see me now? See me now, Hook?

JOHN

Annie, you're flying! You're really flying!

PETER PAN

I'm not Ann—
I'm Pan!
Peter Pan!

*She crows.*

WENDY

Peter! What was death like?

MICHAEL

Does consciousness persist after all?

PETER PAN

It was flying! It was wonderful!

*She crows.*

PETER PAN

Oh I'm light!
Light as air!

HOOK

Peter Pan!
How the devil did you elude my grasp?

*Hook is disoriented.*
*The rest of the children fight him down.*

HOOK

Peter Pan, you rascal!

PETER PAN

Make him walk the plank!

*Michael fights a duel with Hook.*

MICHAEL

I'm fighting a pirate! I'm fighting a pirate!

PETER PAN

Get him, Michael!

*Michael and John have Hook by the throat.*

WENDY

We must show mercy!

PETER PAN

No mercy! Throw him overboard! Slit his throat!

*Michael slits Hook's throat.*

MICHAEL

I killed a pirate. And it was wonderful!

*Wendy bawls.*

WENDY

You killed my brother! I want to go home!

MICHAEL

You're too old for the nursery now, Wendy. I killed a pirate!

PETER PAN

Look at me, way up high!
I'm flying.
The terror is gone.
The sense of flight—weightless!

*A painted drop comes down representing Davenport, Iowa, with
the Mississippi River and the bridge.
Twinkling lights.*

PETER PAN

I can see everything! Davenport, Iowa!
The lights on the Mississippi River!
Oh!

*She crows.*

PETER PAN

Where's my ship?
Now Wendy, think happy thoughts!

WENDY

I can't think happy thoughts—everyone's dead and I'm getting
old and I have arthritis and you have gout—

PETER PAN

THINK HAPPY THOUGHTS!

WENDY

All right, all right let's see . . . happy thoughts . . .

PETER PAN

Fairy dust!

*Peter Pan sprinkles some fairy dust on Wendy.*
*Wendy starts flying.*

WENDY

Oh, Peter, it's wonderful!

*The boys look up at the girls.*

MICHAEL

We want to fly too.

*A ship rolls onstage.*
*It might be a hospital bed with a pirate flag.*

PETER PAN

Then get on board the *Jolly Roger*!

*Hook looks up, not dead.*

HOOK

Can I come?

PETER PAN

Are you reformed, you scurvy pirate?

HOOK

Yes!

*He takes off his Hook hat and his Hook arm.*

HOOK

See, it was a fake!

PETER PAN

Good, then! Everyone, get on board.
Is everyone on? Michael, John?

EVERYONE

We're on!

*The boys get on board a flying ship.*

PETER PAN

All on board?

EVERYONE

Aye, aye, captain.

PETER PAN

Then let's go! This way! Follow me! Line up. Oldest to youngest.
We go in order.

WENDY

We can't line up, we're flying.

PETER PAN

Fine, we don't go in order.
Is everyone on board?
Think happy thoughts.

*They fly.*

WENDY

Can you see our house? Can you see 111? Can we get back into
the nursery?

PETER PAN

No, Wendy, it was your last night in the nursery.

MICHAEL

And Dad sold the house.

WENDY

He sold the house?

JOHN

He died. And we sold it. We all sold the house.

WENDY

Then where are we going to live?
Where will we have Christmas?
I want to go back! I want to go back in!

MICHAEL

We could at least look through the windows!

WENDY

Oh yes yes! Let's!

*Another painted drop might come down representing a house,*
*111 McClellan Boulevard, Davenport, Iowa.*

*They peer through some windows, flying.*
*Wendy knocks on the windows.*

WENDY

Can we get in through the windows?

JOHN

No. The house isn't ours anymore.

*A pause as this sinks in.*

WENDY

Then where will we go?

JOHN

Back to our grown-up lives, I suppose.

PETER PAN

No, no!

*John, Michael, Wendy, and Hook sadly detach their flying cables*
*and go back to being 2, 3, 4, and 5.*

5

We must, Peter. I just remembered that I have a job. With people who are sad, who need me. And also my husband—my two kids— they need me too—

PETER PAN

Don't leave, Wendy!

5

I must, Peter.

3

I have to go cut cancer out of people's bodies. Also I have two grandchildren who I like to hold. I need to go.

2

I have my students. My kids. I need to see my wife. We want to grow old together.

PETER PAN

No, don't leave!

4

I have my patients, my wife, my children. Peter Pan, we can't stay.

*They wave goodbye.*

PETER PAN

When will I see you?
Don't go, don't go!
Oh Wendy!

5

Spring cleaning, Peter Pan!
I'll come back for spring cleaning!

*5 and Peter Pan embrace.*
*Then 5 leaves. She waves goodbye.*

PETER PAN

Ugh. Grown-ups. Spring cleaning. I want to keep flying!

*Peter Pan keeps flying. She sees something.*

PETER PAN

There's the Davenport Children's Theatre!
There's the balcony! There's Mr. Smee! Bump Heeter. My God,
Mary Ellen Hurlbutt—she looks so pretty! And in the audience,
Mary Fluhrer Nighswander! And all the men in the lobby are
wearing hats!

*Peter Pan lands on the stage.*

PETER PAN

I think I see my father in the audience.
I take a bow.

*She takes a bow.*
*Her father approaches.*
*With a bouquet of flowers.*

PETER PAN

Thanks, Dad. Did you grow these yourself?

GEORGE

Yep.
You looked great up there.
How 'bout my little girl flying?
Now let's go back to 111. There's a little party for you.
Mother made Chex party mix.
You can change out of those green tights and come home.

PETER PAN

I can go home?

GEORGE

Whaddya mean, of course you can. It's your last Christmas before
you go out east to college.

We're all going to miss you. But it's going to be an awfully big adventure.

PETER PAN

Do you think so?

GEORGE

I know so.

PETER PAN

I'm suddenly afraid.
Did you die?
What was it like?
Your breathing was terrible.
It seemed like you didn't want to go.
Was it awful?

GEORGE

Come on now, change your costume.

PETER PAN

I don't want to change costumes.

GEORGE

Those green tights can't be too comfortable after a while. Mother's waiting at home.

PETER PAN

Will you come with me?

GEORGE

They don't want a father in the dressing room.

PETER PAN

No, I mean will you come with me?

*A pause.*

GEORGE

Course I will. I've been here all along.

PETER PAN

Oh, good! Will you hold my flowers while I change? And my photograph with Mary Martin?
It's my good luck charm.

*He nods and takes them.*
*A moment.*

GEORGE

I'm very proud of you, Annie.

PETER PAN

Thanks, Dad.

GEORGE

All right.

*They embrace.*
*He exits. She watches him go.*

## Epilogue

PETER PAN

*(To the audience)* And I went up to my dressing room while he
waited.
I took off my green tights.

But before I went home,
I stayed in the theater for a little while longer.
Where you don't have to grow up.

*Music.*
*She throws a handful of pixie dust.*
*It catches the light.*
*She flies off.*
*A fantastical exit.*
*The end.*

# Relics and Acknowledgments

Special thanks to the inimitable Les Waters and Actors Theatre of Louisville for commissioning this play and nurturing it with such love and care. Thank you to Tony Taccone and Berkeley Repertory Theatre, Sandy Shinner and Shattered Globe, and Jessica Thebus for the gift. Thank you to Tim Sanford and Adam Greenfield. Thank you to Scott J., Ellen M., and Charley S. for being part of the extended family. Thank you to the amazing company (Keith, David, Lisa, Ron, Kathy, Danny) that has felt like a family for almost three years. Flying with Kathy Chalfant— how did I get to be so lucky???

Most importantly, thank you to my MOM—who allowed me to tell parts of her story, and then played herself with such honesty, charm, wit, and bravery in Chicago at the Shattered Globe Theatre. I'm not sure how we got away with this art/life trickery— I think it is because we've been playing tricks on art and life ever since I can remember.

I quoted J. M. Barrie's novel *Peter and Wendy* three times and indicated the quotes with quotation marks. The following are photographs from my mother's collection.

Finally, how to acknowledge the contribution of the Kehoe family (Betsy, Bill, Joe, John, in reverse birth order) to this play? Acknowledge is a cold, formal, and inadequate word for their warmth, love, and willingness. How do stories come through families with love, and how do families come through stories with love? It is a mystery. All I know is that I had the good fortune to be born into a great family with stories and talk sailing down all the bannisters, and in such a family, I never felt alone.

*Mary Martin and Kathleen Kehoe Ruhl, my mother, in a dressing room at the Orpheum in Davenport, Iowa, circa 1959.*

# PETER PAN

*Flying Your Way*

**Masonic Temple Auditorium**

**DAVENPORT**

## Friday Evening, Dec. 19, 7:30 p.m.

## Saturday Matinee, Dec. 20 2:00 p.m.

**Presented By Davenport Park Recreation Board**

**CHILDREN'S THEATRE**

**ADMISSION: Season Ticket - Adult or Student 25c**

**Sponsored By: KAABA TEMPLE, A. A. O. N. M. S.**

*Sarah learns to juggle in rehearsal.*
*Drawing by Ron Crawford.*

*Danny, Keith, Lisa, and Kathleen march to Neverland.*
*Drawing by Ron Crawford.*

SARAH RUHL's plays include *How to Transcend a Happy Marriage*; *For Peter Pan on her 70th birthday*; *The Oldest Boy*; *In the Next Room or the vibrator play* (Pulitzer Prize finalist, Tony Award nominee for Best New Play); *The Clean House* (Susan Smith Blackburn Prize, Pulitzer Prize finalist); *Passion Play* (PEN America Award, Fourth Freedom Forum Playwriting Award from The Kennedy Center); *Orlando*; *Late: a cowboy song*; *Dear Elizabeth*; *Dead Man's Cell Phone* (Helen Hayes Award); *Eurydice*; and *Stage Kiss*. She is a two-time Pulitzer Prize finalist and a Tony Award nominee. Her plays have been produced on Broadway at the Lyceum Theatre by Lincoln Center; Off-Broadway at Playwrights Horizons, Second Stage Theater, and at Lincoln Center's Mitzi Newhouse Theater. Her plays have been produced regionally all over the country and have also been produced internationally and translated into over twelve languages. Ms. Ruhl received her MFA from Brown University where she studied with Paula Vogel. She has received the Steinberg Distinguished Playwright Award, the Susan Smith Blackburn Prize, the Whiting Writers' Award, the Lilly Award, a PEN/Laura Pels Award for American Playwright in Mid-career, and the MacArthur "Genius" Award. Her book of essays, *100 Essays I Don't Have Time to Write*, was published by Faber and Faber was a *Times* Notable Book of the Year. She teaches at the Yale School of Drama and lives in Brooklyn with her family.